Praise fc
LIMEHA

GW00467569

"It's the best debut collection I've read in ages. This delightful, nostalgic book is a love letter to Vicky's grandparents. The poems are clever and beautiful..."

Elaine Cusack, *Culture, The Journal*

"The book rolls out with a joyous panache... There is a gorgeous childlike voice to these poems, peppered with songs, rhymes and humour."

Robin Houghton, *Envoi*

"...the language is simple, there is an immediacy here, a freshness... It illustrates Arthurs' gift for tenderness, which is so powerfully demonstrated in this collection."

Paul Blake, *Brittle Star*

"With its lyrical form, the poetry is inspired by childhood memory... beautifully presented..."

Mslexia: Indie Presses

Limehaven is available in other formats:

Audiobook

Ebook

Join Vicky Arthurs' mailing list at:

www.vickyarthurs.com/newsletter

LIMEHAVEN

Vicky Arthurs

Illustrated by Kate Heiss

cedar
bird

This edition published by Cedarbird, 2017
First published in the UK by IRON Press, 2015

Poems/text © Vicky Arthurs 2015
Cover art/illustrations © Kate Heiss 2015
Author photo © Donna-Lisa Healy 2015

A CIP catalogue record for this book is available from
the British Library.

ISBN 978-1-912340-00-2

Typesetting and cover design by David Whitfield
Printed by Lightning Source

Cedarbird
PO Box 348
Newcastle upon Tyne
NE6 9BU

www.cedarbirdbooks.com

CONTENTS

Outdoors

After

For Jack, Mark, Kimm and my cousins
Wendy, Nick and Caroline.

In memory of my grandparents,
May and Charles Austin.

Introduction

These poems are inspired by my grandparents and by memories of the idyll they created at their bungalow 'Limehaven'. My grandfather was a butcher who lived through two World Wars, though he fought in neither. Shaped by wartime, my grandparents were almost self-sufficient. My grandfather hoed and dug, while my grandmother stewed, baked, bottled and preserved.

Their home was a haven, their garden a place of wonder and discovery. Borders brimmed with blooms. Fish slid beneath the surface of the ornamental pond. A lush lawn gave way to apple trees, raspberry canes, gooseberry bushes and row upon row of vegetables.

Here we watched birds build their nests and listened to their chicks peeping in the hedges. We pulled potatoes from the earth and tasted fresh-picked fruit. Indoors, we gobbled sausages from willow-pattern plates and lapped up my nan's stewed apple and custard. We played card games and gambled for buttons.

I learned the names of things and rolled them round my tongue. They had special words I never heard at home – barometer, antimacassar, chrysanthemum, forty winks. They seemed to me exotic – as lovely and perfumed as the roses bulging beyond the lattice window.

My grandparents were not born to this Eden. They created it with love and graft. My nan was the sixth of eleven children. She grew up in Peckham, in a rented flat above a shop. Her father died of tuberculosis when she was 11, and she looked after her younger brothers and sisters while her mother went out to work. Perhaps this was why she was so patient with us when we were little. She never tired of spinning coins across a table or building castles from a pack of cards.

My granddad was a Brixton lad, the son of a butcher's assistant. He left school, aged 12, to learn his father's trade. He knew how to size up an animal for its meat, how to kill and butcher it. I loved to watch him carve a joint – partly because he fed me tidbits before the meal was served.

When I remember my granddad, I picture him outdoors: digging the garden, tending to the tomatoes, training runner beans on a wigwam or taking me fishing. There was a wildness about him. As a small child, I watched him tickle a fish from the net, then slam its head against a stone. "It's kinder that way," he said.

My granddad had foresight. Unimpressed by Neville Chamberlain's declaration of 'peace for our time', he moved his family out of London in 1938. They settled in Shepperton on the River Thames.

After the War, my grandparents sold their house and bought a newsagent and tobacconist shop in a nearby town. My nan ran the business at first, living once more in cramped quarters above a shop – albeit one that bore her name. My granddad soon joined her and sold fishing tackle alongside the newspapers, sweets and tobacco.

They built a thriving business which they sold in 1960, enabling them to buy 'Limehaven' on its generous plot of land. The shop premises continued to bear my nan's name. From time to time my granddad would take me there to buy wine gums and collect the rent.

My grandparents were generous souls and canny traders. The abundance of good food they enjoyed in their retirement was not restricted to garden produce.

'Uncle' Ted would appear at my grandmother's kitchen door, in cloth cap and bloodstained apron, chewing tobacco and clutching neatly wrapped parcels of meat. The top half of the door opened like a stable. Sausages and Sunday joints were handed in, and jams, pickles, fruit or runner beans were sometimes handed out, depending on the season.

I didn't question these mysterious transactions. They seemed natural – part of the bounty of the place. My cousin has since told me that my granddad offered his expertise to a local butcher in return for a lifetime's supply of meat.

I never revisited 'Limehaven' after my grandparents died. I've heard the house is now a ruin. The roof has been torn off and rain falls where once we clustered round the telly. In time, perhaps, bulldozers will move in and clear the land for new development.

It stands intact in my memory. I've walked once more through its rooms, running my fingers over the furnishings: the coarse cotton antimacassars, the crocheted doilies, the bobbly settee. I've picked up my grandmother's pretty hairbrush and felt the cool glass that topped her dressing table. I've marvelled at the Teasmade, snug beside their bed. I've conjured clocks and chairs, wardrobes and wallpaper, in shimmering 3D.

Bringing my grandparents into focus has been more difficult. Whenever I tried to summon them, they'd beetle off into another room. I'd hear a rattling cup or a chesty cough, or catch a whiff of mint rising from a saucepan. Still, I couldn't picture them. In the end, I found them in the fabric of the place.

Some poems grew from remembering rooms or objects. Others took family legends as their starting point. These were sketchy – headline news handed down by unreliable narrators. "Your nan's hair turned white overnight when your granddad got smashed up in a motorbike accident." "Your granddad never went to war."

In fact, my grandfather volunteered for military service in 1914, joining a battalion of cyclists. But he was never sent overseas. In 1915, his father died and he was discharged to care for his invalid mother. In the Second World War, he was too old to enlist and joined the Home Guard River Patrol.

The ballad *Two wars, two sons* grew from awkward memories of watching Remembrance Day services on the telly: poppy petals swirling down like blood-spattered snow, while my granddad shook silently. I felt compelled to give voice to all he left unsaid, but, of course, that voice turned out to be mine.

That's the trouble with writing about people you love. You strive to be true to them, but the poems take on a life of their own. I offer them, not as a record, but as a tribute: to two people whose love was as abundant as the wonders of their garden.

Before

Courting Mabel

He swallowed the moon for an Adam's apple;
She shattered her teeth on a mouthful of stars.
Shyness and brightness, their hearts beating fast,
A billion yesterdays lighting their path.

Two wars, two sons

The boy who wields the butcher's knife
Never went to war.
And not for want of wanting to,
Nor conscience, he forbore;
But still he chose the slaughterhouse
And never went to war.

The boy who wears his father's steel
Never wore a gun,
Never marched to glory,
Never shot the Hun.
His battlefront is nearer home,
A crippled widow's son.

Oh, do not go to war, my son!
Do not go to war!
Do not fight and do not die!
Do not go to war!

He walks among the women folk,
Defies their tear-stained eyes,
Shouldering the carrion,
The boy who stayed behind.

He'll not be called a coward
Or a lily-livered lad:
His bloodstained apron weeps of beasts,
He works at Death's right hand.

Yet in the tangled dark he dreams
Where waking soldiers walk,
The human bellow of the bull:
The dying of their screams.

Oh, do not go to war, my son!
Do not go to war!
Do not fight and do not die!
Do not go to war!

A generation went to war;
A generation died.
He waited, hopeful, for his friends,
But few came back alive.

The few came back, returned as ghosts,
As though they too were gone.
Behind their eyes, the horrors
Of the slaughter on the Somme.

Caught in a remembrance
They knew not how to tell,
That licked them from the inside out:
A livid, present hell.

Do not go to war, my son!
Do not go to war!
Do not fight and do not die!
Do not go to war!

II

The boy who did not go to war
Was saved to have a son,
And bonny was the butcher's lad
Who grew to be a man.

But time the parson, time the thief,
Was counting, all those years,
A tithe on that uneasy peace
Accrued in human fears.

And monsters born of battle
And violated ghosts
Called down devastation
Upon their human hosts.

The drums of war are beating now,
The drums of war are near.
The drums, the drums! Send forth your sons!
The drums of war are near.

"Oh, spare my lad and in his stead
I'll fight your bloody war,
Though it besmirch the memory
Of those who fought before."

"The bayonet, the butcher's knife
Are not so far apart:
Their metal sings of mettle,
Though the latter has more art."

"I've seen the bloody slaughterhouse,
I've slain the bloody bull;
I've mopped the floor of blood and gore,
I'm not afraid to fight your war!"

"But do not send my son, my God!
Do not send my son!
Let me fight and let me die!
But do not send my son!"

"We do not doubt your skill, old mate,
We do not doubt your front,
But you're too old for modern war
And youth must bear the brunt."

So, father now, the butcher boy
Must face the call to arms,
Quite powerless to save his son,
Whom he would shield from harm.

"If you must fight, best fly a plane
And soar above the rest,
Than wade toward Death in mud and blood,
A bullet in your chest."

And so he sends his son to war.
He sends his son to war.
With blessings in his shredded heart,
He sends his son to war.

Now Charles patrols the Home Front;
Son Charlie flies the skies.
Dad mans the anti-aircraft guns
And something in him dies:

In every German bomber plane,
There sits a German son,
A frightened lad in uniform,
Beloved of his Mum.

"They take you young, they spill your blood –
Whatever is it for?
For in another twenty years
They'll send your sons to war!"

Do not go to war, my son!
Do not go to war!
Let's be done with lost and won.
Do not go to war!

Charlie came home safe from war.
His father, doubly blessed,
Carried with him all his life
The wounds of all the rest.

Milk and moonshine

Her love is the colour of milk and moonshine,
White and wet as a broken bone.
She flutters at dusk in a darkened window,
Her hands untethered, her hair undone.

A man on a motorbike pictures her waiting,
Petrol singing in his veins,
"Shatter my bones, I'll always come home to you!"
Muscle to metal, leans into the turn.

Her love is the colour of blackout curtains,
Snuffed out streetlamps, tarmac skies,
Hooded headlights, hubs colliding,
Night-roosting ravens startled in scores.

Tendon and sinew entangle with metal,
Spinning his wheels, as she waits through the night.
Tibia, fibula burst into nebulae,
Nerves on fire, he's fading to nought.

Alone in a ditch by a rain-sluiced lane,
Where hawthorn twigs impale the stars,
Caught in his throat, the song of the raven,
Wings pinned by the weight of her dread.

Her love is the colour of milk and moonshine,
Wedding veil, christening gown, shimmer of God,
"Outrun the shadows and make your way home..."
She plucks at the sheet on his hospital bed.

Indoors

Welcome

Mabel in her pinafore
giggles through her stable door:
"Not today, thank you!"

Eating her up

She is flour and dumplings,
subtle as peaches,
tart as rhubarb,
sweet as a cherry cake.

Stands in the slipstream of
slow-cooked lunches,
buttoned in her apron,
lovely as a lark.

Scent her in the steam
rising from a colander;
all minted potatoes
and fresh-popped peas.

Catch her in the sunshine
of homegrown tomatoes,
willow-pattern loveliness,
summer on a plate.

She's sausages on Saturdays,
bread and dripping sandwiches,
raspberry ripple ice cream
sliced with a knife.

She's Kilner jars and kindness,
bottled generosity,
Christmas puddin' charity –
homemade Nan.

My grandfather is a country

My grandfather is a country.
Rough terrain. Etched upon his hands
A map. Rivers and roads and feet above sea level,
Contours in the whorls of his fingertips.
He has carved a path across his palm.
I walk my fingers through its valley,
Sensing the mountains all around –
The untamed mountains,
Volcanic, bronchial.

Dominoes

I learn to count
in ebony and ivory,
in tusk and trunk
from jungle lands.

Tumbling to the table,
an avalanche of forest things;
memories of elephants,
pockmarked by pips.

One-eyed ones and timid twos,
threes ascending like a song,
cat's-paw fours and tiger fives;
oh, for a pair of blackberry sixes!

The fall of the monarchy on a Monday afternoon

We launch an armada over the table,
Tenpenny pieces and tuppeny bits,
Flotilla of shillings, spinning, spinning,
Blazing spheres of space and light.
Worlds hypnotic, gyroscopic.
Orbs in motion. Moon and ocean.
Energy, savagery. Waves and gravity.
See how the mighty come clattering down:
Clattering, flattening, turning to sound,
To George – Five, Six – Elizabeth,
Hula-hoop monarchs that rattle and roll.
Imperial, decimal – all die the same:
"Off with their heads, Nanna! Spin them again!"

Hunting for winks

I prowl the soporific hours, hunting for winks.
I stalk them under slumbering chairs,
behind snoring clocks and snoozing ornaments.
"Winks, winks wherever you are…"
They shimmer behind drawn curtains,
flickery as eyelashes. Flit unseen
beneath the aspidistra, too quick to catch.
Sly as haggis, they are. Scarce as monkeys,
pattering across the mantelpiece.

Light slips on sleek tables, dozing in the glow
of afternoon. The sofa is comatose.
A cupboard gapes. A drawer yawns.
The curtain flutters. Something skitters
over the ceiling. There! A glance on mirrored glass.
On your marks, prepare to pounce!

My grandfather opens an eye…
and closes it.
One!

I was promised forty.
They are not fun, these winks –
Not the tiddly kind.

The visitor

teatime visitor
tapping on the leaded lights
a one-eyed robin

Patient pursuits

She has a hundred ways to make me happy.
She builds pagodas out of cards. Leans kings
on courtiers, cloisters them in subtle walls,
lays careful rooves on flimsy villas.
Adds breathless spires. Then claps her hands
and makes them vanish, collapsing palace
into air. We lace the ruins into crosses,
toss them like pancakes.

She feeds me sweets in Lent. Turns saints
to seagulls. Bids them fly from her fingers.
She summons sparrows to her table,
crumbles cake for the blind robin. Builds
a palisade of dominoes and suffers me
to knock it down. We make a windmill
from the rubble. Ivory sails engulf the carpet,
spun from a hub of riveting sixes.

She cuts me a chorus line,
makes printed minstrels dance a jig,
leaves holes in newspapers. She turns heads.
Spins kings and queens till they are giddy.
She shows me how to shuffle; lay bets with buttons;
beat my neighbours out of doors; snap
with the best of them. She teaches me patience.
The twelve hours on the clock. Each in its place.

Determining the weather

Grandfather almighty,
Captain of the clouds,
Steer us through the storms
With your aneroid barometer.

Commandeer the compass point,
Swing the sickle moon!
Quell the swelling tempest,
Then summon up the sun!

Nor'easterly, sou'westerly,
Direct the fickle wind:
It does not know which way to blow
Without your brisk command.

Your knuckles give the ordinance,
Sound bone on sacred glass,
Bend elements to instrument,
Your word will come to pass.

Speak to me of millibars
And mystic incantations,
Fahrenheit and centigrade,
Alchemical dimensions.

Teach me how to take the helm,
Be skipper of the skies,
Plot a course from rain to change,
Or bid a sea fret rise!

"Get behind me, giddy girl,
Dismiss these fiendish notions!
No man commands the firmament,
No mortal moves the oceans!"

Powder puff

Her dressing table is a magic realm:
A fairy-tale hairbrush, a terrible comb,
A delicate web of lace and ice;
Snowflakes and flowers and strands of silver,
A downy duckling in a looking glass.

I follow her face through halls of mirrors,
A kiss, a kiss on her paper skin.
She dabs my nose with a powder puff:
Soft. Soft. Soft as a cygnet.
Scented dust: its sunlit beauty.

You knit the ocean

You knit him an ocean, wave on wave,
A mustard ship on a bottle-green sea,
Cracked leather buttons and barrels of brandy,
We'll weather the evening, him, you an' me.

Cast on, cast off, from Jersey to Guernsey,
A skein of gold in your treasure chest,
The swell of the wool, the pull of the needle,
Your mind is your compass, your hands do the rest.

Billowing sleeves and rope-tangled rigging,
A blight on the stitch that drops out of sight!
You sail undaunted into the evening,
Eyes fixed on the star-studded night.

I'm diving for purls in a swirling ocean,
Riding the waters where dreams swim free,
I voyage on your needles – they carry me, carry me,
Carry my coracle far out to sea.

What's in a name

There are names that taste of teatime –
Parkinson's and Parker Knoll –
of cakes in pleated cases
and cool thick milk.

There are sounds that sing of coconut –
the unchecked rattle of her cup,
the tremble of her tea plate,
her terrified spoon.

Thanks be to TV

The cathode rays burn bright tonight.
We bathe in phosphorescent light,
Like whey-faced worshippers at prayer,
We sit, we sup, we sigh, we stare.

Our mother's stopped misquoting Marx –
No "opiate", no "masses' fix" –
She gazes, chastened and serene,
As Robert Mitchum steals the scene.

We have no TV in the week,
So Saturday's a Sabbath feast:
We gorge ourselves on starry light,
On minstrels painted black and white,

On Brucie's banter, Beadle's games,
On bright new faces seeking fame,
On Time Lords, Daleks, dancing girls,
On Ironside's wheels, on Starsky's curls…

This orb through which our heroes pass,
This miracle of light and glass,
This oracle of playground cool
Will keep us safe all week at school.

Company

Dust the clocks! Company's coming!
Starch the doilies and summon the chairs!
Fire the oven and bake like a demon!
Out with the elbow grease, on with the chores!

Enter the shaded room at noon,
Throw wide the curtains and scatter the sun,
Risk the fading of the sofa,
Pummel the cushions and beat the rugs!

Dusters skate on polished mahogany,
Rainbow feathers tickle the heights,
Particles storm in glorious sunbeams –
Diamond shafts through leaded lights.

Lay the table we never eat at,
Put out the china we never use,
Polish the glasses that nobody drinks from,
Answer the doorbell that nobody rings!

Jovial voices boom in the hallway.
She carries their coats. He shows off the bar.
Optics and measures, a corner of heaven,
"Sherry or Babycham? Guinness or beer?"

Company II

Company comes
among the Capodimontes,
rumpling the antimacassars.

Sleeping with ghosts

What is spare about a room?
The empty bed where Dolly died,
The eiderdown in weeds of green,
The Teasmade stopped at ten to twelve,
The virgin candle on the shelf.
I'm not saying I'm scared,
But there are dead coats in the wardrobe
And strangers in the chest of drawers.

Mysteries

Don't lock yourself in!

Vic's vapour rub and TCP
Pumice and a coral sponge
Suckers on a rubber bathmat
Armitage Shanks

Shiny bolt or ancient key –
Which is it to be?

Nick and the beanstalk

The ladder is a beanstalk
into another world:
carpeted with light,
furnished with possibility.

Long-legged cousins,
soon taller than the house,
lie coiled like beansprouts
waiting for the rain.

The song of the knife

How does he bid the knife to sing?
Bowing the meat like a violin,
Delicate slices, the tenderest cuts –
See the love! Blood! Love in the knife!

What does it sing of, the keening knife?
The sting of the steel? The loss of a life?
The scars on his fingers, the nicks in his heart?
See the love! Blood! Love in the knife!

Who forged the knife that could hold a tune?
Who whet its edge on a wheel of stone?
Who dreamed its blade from the heart of the fire?
Who saw blood, love? Blood on the knife.

Wildebeest, buffalo, flint and savannah,
Running the bull to death or dishonour,
Hoof-drum and heartbeat, the panicking herd.
The hunter. The hunted. The blood on the knife.

King of the feast, how he makes the knife sing,
A rebel, a revel, a roundel, a ring!
Artistry, butchery meet in his hands –
See the love! Blood! Love in the man!

Eager for Easter

She keeps it hidden in a paper bag,
beribboned beauty: the perfect egg.
A flash of foil – a glimpse of gold and emerald –
springtime colour shimmering on its shell.

Watch me weigh its secrets in my hand,
shake the cocoa embryo that wakes within!
Two flawless halves will open like a mussel,
split like a lily bud, flowering in my palms.

I dream a waft of milk and vanilla pod,
sugar cane and cocoa bean perfuming my skin –
see glittering within, a razzle-dazzle treasure trove,
and folded in the foil, the creases of her smile.

Outdoors

Blackbird

solo blackbird
on the TV aerial
broadcasting his song

May bells in the borderlands

On the shadow side of the bungalow,
Where I'm not supposed to play,
Lies a gloomy path where the firs crowd in
And the villainous ivy chokes the day.

A forbidding and forbidden place
By a fence that's tall and steep:
I creep on the path where the sun never comes
And the grass grows damp and deep.

We hide and seek through this lonely land
Where a child can run to ground.
Her trembling voice drifts away on the wind
And I fear I will not be found.

I can hear the thudding of her heart
Through the rough and eyeless wall,
But something makes me stay where I am:
Something knotted, tear-choked, small.

Beyond stands a gate in a whitewashed arch
Where the iron is wrought with light,
Where shadows play in the borderlands
And the fields beyond glow bright.

I have heard them whisper to the walls
Of children disappeared,
Still I slink to the gate where her demons wait:
The fulfilment of her fears.

Almost there…do I dare? Do I dare?
My hand on the dainty latch.
What's to fear? All is beauty here.
All is light, all is bright…slip the catch…

Then a shrieking magpie streaks from the sky,
Torn wings and rattling dread:
"Oh Child take flight, it's a limbic light
And it shines on the lost and the dead!"

Stumbling back down the tangled track,
I thrash through the smothering trees,
Till, blinded by tears and her shapeless fears,
I slip and fall to my knees.

As I sink in the soft and spongy moss,
A spray of teardrops springs from the ground:
Here Eve left Eden and wept for her loss,
Here a peal of May bells makes no sound.

Here's a heady scent of heaven spent,
Here a virgin cried for shame,
Here a saint and a dragon mingled blood,
And the lily bears her name.

Little blighter

under the netting
beak bloodied with raspberries
a lone sparrow feasts

Reflection

My grandfather, the heron, stands slow:
legs rooted in the rockery, wind
ruffling his crest. Listens to the slip
of pond on stone, as he skims the willow
from the water. An artist with the net,
he skirts the lily pads, passing the time
with water boatmen, while shimmering sky
ripples to the rhythm of his breath,
and big-lipped fish mouth slow hellos
on the underside of the looking glass.

Earthworm

Lobby, Lobby, Lobby Lud
Chewing through your weight in mud

Glistening in the fresh-turned earth
Terrible in length and girth

Prince of earthworms, lordly slug
Purple, naked and undug

Grotesque and giant annelid
Slither slowly whence you slid!

(A robin perching on a spade
Looks on, songless and amazed.)

Treasures

He shows me treasures:

the broken blue
of a blackbird's egg;

a bean seed
in the palm of his hand;

the green swelling
of a new tomato;

a velvet apricot;
a lobby lud.

Greenhouse

baked terracotta
seedling trays on wooden slats
we breathe tomatoes

Tortoise wars

He is torn from the heat
of the compost heap.
My mother turns him upside down
to sex him.

It's all wrong – a foreign finger,
bones on the inside,
tracing the scoop
of his smooth shell.

Reptile blink
finds the sky turned green,
till the world
rights itself with dizzying velocity.

Strange claws
scrape at his carapace,
counting the rings
on his every scute.

"Why, he's forty, fifty, seventy, a hundred!"

Treading air,
he ponders the indignity,
recoils at fresh atrocities,
hissing his revenge.

Feet touch earth,
now he swims through the couch grass,
lurching through the undergrowth
in khaki combat camouflage.

We find him later,
charging through the cloche,
gums blazing,
ravaging the lettuces.

On top of the willow

On top of the willow, on top of the world!
I sit on a plateau of tangled strands.
Sinewy tendrils encircle my hands
As bungalows tilt at a difficult sky.

On top of the willow, on top of the world!
Plum trees spin through the icy blue.
Orbiting fruit, like myriad moons,
Beyond my reach as they hurtle by.

On top of the willow, on top of the world!
Dizzying distances shrink and grow –
The pond rears up from far below,
Recedes to a puddle, then swims out of sight.

How did I land on this perilous nest?
A shoulder, a ladder, a fireman's lift:
A daredevil uncle who threw me aloft,
A daredevil granddad who deemed it wise.

I sail alone on a roiling swell,
Where chimneys teeter and aerials lurch,
Brushing the wings of startled birds,
As rooftops reel from my staring eye.

My cousin before me travelled these skies,
Her hair aflame, her arms unfurled –
On top of the willow, on top of the world!
I smile for the camera and try not to cry.

Heatwave

The soil has turned to ash, no wind to stir it.
Sparrows bomb the parched afternoon,
scooping hollows in the dust.

They lather their feathers – puff
and wallow, flutter and shudder –
seeking relief in a desert storm.

The fountain has been silent all summer.
Ants clamber the brown moss,
audible in the scorched lawn.

Last year, rainbows formed in gleaming spray;
we darted, laughing, under angular showers,
sparkling with the thrill of it.

Now we wilt in panting shade.
The willow thirsts. The lilies blaze.

Hear no evil

The stone duck with the broken nose
stands guard beside the pond.
Whitewash peeling,
waggletail rump,
belly green with algae.

Her painted eye sees supple fish
darting gold in dapple-green.
Turns a concrete ear
to the screams of newts
bludgeoned behind the rockery.

Hook, line and sinker

He takes me fishing in the Wilderness.
The hush of summer simmers under brook
and birdsong as we swish through lush grass:
long strides, pink cheeks, fresh air. We've come prepared:
rod and line and houndstooth cap, lunch box packed
with maggots. A wagtail dips and curtsies.
My granddad tips his cap. He picks this spot,
unfolds his canvas stool and baits his hook.
He casts his line. Whoop! Sing! The reel spins:
a plop, a float bobbing, ripples and silence.
I have promised not to frighten the fish.
The see-through thread hangs in the air
like bad magic.

Requiem for a fish

He thrashes on the bank, drowning in air.
He leaps and flip-flaps, scales flash silver:
one last dance with the light.

He's swimming for his life:
battering his body from the earth to a sea
of nothing.

So light. So much nothing. He swims on
into the void. Who'd have thought oblivion
as giddy as this?

After

He broke his heart like Jesus

He broke his heart like Jesus:
It burst within his chest,
And all the love and all the blood
Welled up within his breast.

A heart that stirred, a heart that roared,
A heart that loved so well,
Lies broken now, its absent beat
A cracked and silent bell.

They say he didn't suffer,
His ancient bones stood strong,
But still his broken heart remains,
A heart that loved so long.

He broke his heart like Jesus:
They pierced his side to see,
And blood and water flowed without,
A rising tide set free.

A rising tide to sail the soul,
To sail the soul to sea.
His broken heartbeat, distant now,
But echoing in me.

Life cycle

May is born in September:
into a sea of Michaelmas daisies,
under the apple's fruiting bough;
onto a bed of bloodied geraniums,
bald as a poppy head, flawed as a rose.
Naked as an Autumn crocus,
nursed in the garden's embrace;
wrapped in a membrane, sequined with honesty,
honeysuckling Nature's breast.

May is married in July:
crowned with lily of the valley,
heart ablaze with unseeded delight;
glimpsing a garden yet to be planted:
riotous flowerbeds, rose-scented nights.
Arm in arm at the altar of summer,
Solomon's splendour dimmed by her smile;
rivers of peonies flood through her fingers,
zinnias sing her down the aisle.

May gives birth to January.
Knows the secret life of soil,
bulbs dividing in the dark.
Bears the labour pains of winter,
clutching ivy, biting bark;
Christmas rose, a crown of holly,
blood and sweat upon her brow.
Stab of joy. The firstborn snowdrops
shoulder through the frozen ground.

May begets a gentle summer,
lilac-eyed and butterfly bright.
Dancing wild in bee-tickled lavender:
joy unbound in humming spires.
Blush of plums, abundant autumn;
windfalls, wasps, all honey-drunk,
can't dismay her unsung Eden
bearing fruit at heaven's brink.

May lies down to die in March:
numb to frost on shards of grass.
Translucent, veined, a crocus petal
withered by a bitter blast.
Longer days cast deeper shadows,
brimstone wings eclipse the light.
She coils inside herself like bracken
born again from winter's night.

She crochets the stars

Knit me a lullaby
Knit me to sleep
Knit me the night-time
Soft and deep

Crochet the stars
With your dainty hook
Knit me some counting sheep
Knit me a crook

Spin me a story
Spin me the moon
Spin me the milky way
Sleep will come soon

Wrap me in starlight
And indigo lace
Wrap me in silence
Wrap me in space

Weave me a basket
Filled with dreams
Weave it with riversong
Fished from a stream

And in the morning
Prove it was you –
Crochet a cobweb
Decked with dew.

Leaving Limehaven

Night above the bungalow.
Stars crowd in. The universe
contained within her garden.

Voices float beneath the lime.
The air is pregnant with sighs.
Time, time – I would hold back time –
stretching the moment before goodbye.
I am. I am. I am. I am…

…perfumed roses by the drive,
glow-worms glimpsed through sleepy eyes,
fading fences, moonlit gravel,
my grandmother's footsteps
disappearing.

May and Charles Austin (1922)

Acknowledgements

Many thanks to:

My brothers, cousins and Auntie Pat for answering questions about tall tales my mother told me.

Artist Kate Heiss, designer David Whitfield and photographer Donna-Lisa Healy – my creative visual dream team.

Everyone who lent their time and talents to help these poems find an audience, especially Peter Mortimer at IRON Press, who believed in the book and published the first UK print edition.

My family and friends for their support and encouragement – and, above all, my husband Jack.

About the author

Vicky Arthurs is a writer, editor and performer. She is inspired by nature and creates poetry that celebrates everyday life. Her work was first published by IRON Press. She performs at festivals and events and has recorded *Limehaven* as an audiobook. Vicky has worked in television, training and publishing. She ran her own business in the personal development sector for ten years and enjoys helping people unlock their creative talents.

www.vickyarthurs.com

About the illustrator

Kate Heiss graduated from the Royal College of Art in Textile Design in 1997 and worked as a textile designer for several major fashion brands. In 2011, Kate set up her own printmaking studio after studying at the Curwen Studio. Kate's linocuts are inspired by her love of nature.

www.kateheiss.com

Lightning Source UK Ltd.
Milton Keynes UK
UKOW04f0841100817
307037UK00002B/59/P